Our Socially Awkward Marriage

Stories from an Adult Relationship on the Asperger's End of the Autism Spectrum

TOM PETERS

AND

LINDA PETERS

Our Socially Awkward Marriage

Tom Peters and Linda Peters

Published by Brookside Press

ISBN-13: 978-0-9842230-3-9

CONTENTS

Knowledge is of no value unless you put it into practice.

--Anton Chekhov

INTRODUCTION

Remember that weird kid in the back of the classroom who just couldn't stop talking about astronomy, and would bring up the discovery of Pluto during lessons about the American Civil War? That was me.

My name is Tom Peters. I'm a composer and GRAMMY®-nominated classical musician now, and I've played music all over the world. I have a wife named Linda, a college-aged son from my first marriage, and eight different types of stringed instruments at home including six ukuleles. In 2011, at the tender age of 47, I was diagnosed with Asperger's Syndrome.

At that time, Asperger's Syndrome was considered a mild form of autism, characterized by an inability to understand how to interact socially. Those of us with Asperger's -- or Aspies, as a term of endearment -- tend to have few facial expressions and are apt to stare blankly at other people. It's nothing personal; we really can't help it.

Aspies are often accused of being "in their own world" and preoccupied with their own thoughts. We are usually clumsy with uncoordinated movements, are socially awkward, have repetitive routines or rituals, and odd speech and language.

Which didn't exactly make me a chick magnet.

Regardless of an Aspie's age or place in life, relationships are often a challenge. Being unable to understand nonverbal communication or how you relate to the people around you can cause Aspies to blurt out inappropriate remarks and say just plain odd things, usually at exactly the wrong time.

Although Asperger's Syndrome was lumped into the more general diagnosis of Autism Spectrum Disorder in 2013, my condition remains the same, regardless of the label. I still have the same symptoms. I am still the same person. In the privacy of my own home, and in the pages of these stories, I still refer to myself as having the diagnosis formerly known as Asperger's Syndrome.

But it's not all bad news. The unusual focus and intensity that goes along with this disorder has helped me to hone my skills as a professional double bass player and later, as a composer of silent film scores. On a personal level, I am honest, dependable and straightforward. I love deeply and always try to do my best. I don't play mind games. I don't know how.

And now, as a middle-aged adult, I'm in a happy, healthy relationship. My wife, Linda, is a writer who used to work with adults with mental, emotional and developmental disabilities. It was Linda's idea for me to share some anecdotes about what it feels like to be on the high-functioning end of the autism spectrum. She thought it might help someone to hear me articulate the feelings involved in some of the unique challenges I face. Around the same time, we also started writing articles together about how we were making communication work so well in our Asperger's relationship.

This book is a collection of some of those articles and blog posts about our lives. Most of the stories are about being on the spectrum, or about living with someone who is on the spectrum. Almost all the stories take place in the context of our Asperger's relationship and subsequent marriage. We hope that you enjoy reading them!

HOW TOM AND I MET

In hindsight, maybe a grunion run wasn't the best choice for one of my first dates with a man that I'd met online. Tom and I were holding hands in the dark auditorium of the Cabrillo Marine Aquarium, watching a nature film about spawning fish. It was kind of awkward. But the early stages of a new relationship usually are.

I had met Tom on Chemistry.com, prior to the advent of GPS-enabled smartphone dating apps, back before Tinder was even a glimmer in a coder's eye. It was the dark ages, when you had to scroll through dating profiles at home, after work, with a glass of wine and a desktop computer.

Chemistry was Match.com's answer to eHarmony, and it required you to take a comprehensive personality test before being matched with a handful of potential coffee dates. It was designed for online daters who were serious about finding a long-term relationship, who believed that a series of psychologically probing multiple choice questions could improve the odds of a successful match, and who were jumping back into the dating pool in their forties.

Tom and I both wrote in our online profiles that the ocean was important to us. We both liked fish, nature and marine mammals. And so our courtship took place on whale watching boats, on a deserted boardwalk surrounded by sea birds at the Bolsa Chica wetlands, and staring down at bright orange Garibaldi on Catalina Island. In a way, a grunion run made perfect sense in the context of our evolving relationship.

When we decided it was time to become exclusive, we giddily changed our Facebook statuses to "In a Relationship." Then we pledged to deactivate our dating profiles.

"I met someone!" I told Chemistry, through a drop-down menu of reasons to unsubscribe. Chemistry gave me a half-hearted send-off, letting me know that even though I was leaving them, they would still save my account information so it would be there if I ever wanted to come back. "Just in case it doesn't work out," seemed to be Chemistry's passive-aggressive parting shot.

But when Tom tried to unsubscribe, he was pressured hard to stay. "We have other great singles in your area," Chemistry told Tom, trying to distract him from the unsubscribe button. "Have you seen your new matches? Here's Evelyn from Temple City!" Tom continued to delete his account. "Are you sure?" the site asked once again, with just a hint of malice.

In today's world, love has to triumph over e-commerce, over marketing tactics designed to make you feel dissatisfied. Love has to overpower those carefully-crafted suggestions intended to lure you back to monthly subscription fees and serial dating.

To be happy, we have to learn to trust our instincts over external messages. Because in the end, online dating is not all that different from grunion love. Those slender silvery fish, twerking on the sand, have left their comfort zones with a primal goal in mind. They are looking for a mate. And, as scores of grunion make love in the moonlight, they serve as a visual representation of the idea that there are still plenty of fish in the sea. And maybe sometimes a digital device is just the thing we need to help us find the right one.

SQUEEZING PUGS

Tom says: For a good portion of my adult life, I have been convinced that pugs can go to the bathroom only when squeezed. This notion came from my early adult days in Chicago. My friend Jeff rented a room from a family in Evanston during his time at Northwestern University, and one of the conditions of his stay was that he was to take care of George, the family pug. George had some issues; the worst of which was that his bowels didn't work properly and he needed some help. It was Jeff's job to squeeze him.

I often kept Jeff company on his walks with the dreaded George, so after the initial shock of seeing a pug thoroughly squeezed wore off, I assumed—like the good little Aspie that I am—that *all* pugs needed to be squeezed.

Shortly after I met Linda, George somehow came into the conversation. I professed to Linda that although they are cute, pugs have a certain maintenance problem. I'm not sure how to accurately describe the look I got in return.

Linda says: I was telling Tom that I thought pugs were cute. It was an offhand comment based on a friend's Facebook post. I wasn't planning on getting a dog at that time. But Tom looked concerned. He advised me not to get a pug, and then he told me why.

I'm not an expert on pugs but it seemed unlikely that the smiling women dressing pugs up in Christmas sweaters for Instagram pictures were okay with this whole squeezing thing. So I turned to Google and punched in a variety of rather unsavory keywords. And after a fair amount of research, I could find no evidence that Tom's claim about the entire pug breed had any merit at all.

And thus, the term "pug-squeezing" was born. Any generalization made on the basis of a single experience -- something that Tom can be prone to do -- has since been met with this pointed question: Honey, are you squeezing a pug?

In our relationship, we've found that communication works best when it is clear and direct. But when referring to situations involving potential pug poo, it also helps to keep things light and playful.

We've read a lot online about how difficult relationships on the Autism spectrum can be. How burdensome it is for the neurotypical, or non-Asperger's partner. We've been advised by scholarly articles that our relationship will be problematic, and will quite possibly fail. But we seem to be doing just fine -- in fact, a lot of the time, we're downright giddy. To us, the whole notion that neurologically mixed marriages are inherently unworkable is no better than squeezing a pug.

LINDA'S ADVICE FOR COMMUNICATING WITH AN ASPIE PARTNER: BE LITERAL

Tom and I had just moved into a new apartment and my future stepson had left his dirty dishes next to the sink. Again.

"Can you please show him how the dishwasher works?" I said to Tom. It wasn't really an accusation. The place that he and his son had lived before was dishwasher-free.

I went out the door to collect the laundry. When I came back, the dishes were still sitting next to the sink, untouched. Tom was watching TV.

"I thought you were going to show him how the dishwasher worked," I said.

"I did."

There had to be more to this story. "What did you say to him?"

Tom opened the dishwasher and pointed inside. "I showed him how the rotating jets ascend when the door is locked, and how the chemical composition and velocity of the arching spray rinses off the food and disinfects the plates." He smiled, like he was proud of his role in passing on the physics of dishwashing to a new generation.

Here's the thing. Tom had explained *how* the dishwasher worked because that is exactly what I had asked him to do.

"I just wanted you both to put your dishes in there," I said. But from Tom's perspective, if that's what I had wanted, why didn't I just say so?

It's hard to believe that a person can be so completely literal. I had thought that everyone understood how to read between the lines and decipher the hidden meaning behind the words. I believed everyone responded to language the same way that I did.

It would have been easy for me to get upset over this situation, and to blame Tom for secretly trying to make me angry by using a "literal loophole" to avoid fulfilling my request. But it's equally easy to believe that my sweetheart is a helpful, loving person who happens to process language differently than I do. And when I approach communication from this perspective, things tend to turn out better. I am able to get my point across clearly and we both get to feel heard and understood.

TOM'S UKULELE OBSESSION
AND OTHER SPECIAL INTERESTS

Ah yes, Asperger's obsessions. Some Aspies have a life-long special interest, such as the Titanic, baseball scores, or Winnie-the-Pooh. Trains and astronomy are biggies. I'm one of those who tend to bounce from one special interest to the next. When I was a kid, it was astronomy, magic and Tchaikovsky. Later on it was marine biology, horticulture and bonsai. As an adult, it has been movies from the silent era, electronic music and John Cage. From my earliest memories to now, music has been a constant thread.

Lately my special interest has become the ukulele. One thing I've been enjoying about discovering the ukulele is how easy it has been to learn, especially after spending so much time playing classical bass professionally for the last 25+ years.

The ukulele has seen a renaissance over the past few years, but it has continually held an important place in popular music. The ease of playing and its portability have had as much to do with its staying power as the warm, gentle tone. In fact, the ukulele got its start as Hawaiian versions of small Portuguese guitars. The legend is that native Hawaiians gravitated to the instrument because it could be easily carried into the fields and played on breaks. It was given its Hawaiian name "ukulele" by the field workers.

The ukulele made an off-island sensation debuting at the Hawaiian Pavilion at the 1915 Panama Pacific International Exposition in San Francisco. Tin Pan Alley composers cashed in on the whole Hawaiian craze that swept the nation by penning exotic island-sounding tunes. The uke caught on, becoming the go-to instrument throughout the first half of the 20th Century until it was knocked off its perch by the guitar in the late 50s. My primary interest is in songs of the 20s and 30s.

I've been playing the ukulele now for about four years and I love it. Frustration has been kept (so far) to a minimum, and I'm really happy with the results. I still have a lot to learn, but it's been great fun discovering well-known and lesser-known Tin Pan Alley and Hawaiian gems.

BRAIN LOCK! A LOOK INSIDE THE INNER WORKINGS OF AN OVER-STIMULATED ASPERGER'S BRAIN

What do you do when your husband freezes in a river full of moving people?

Tom and I were at a flashback 80's rock concert and the Go-Go's had just finished their encore. As we got up to leave the Hollywood Bowl bleacher seats along with thousands of other people, Tom's hand gripped my shoulder.

"Are you all right?" I said.

He gripped harder and we crept toward the exit. I knew something was wrong so I tried to guide him. People were pushing from all sides. It was like rush hour on the 405 Freeway and there was no place to pull over. "We're almost out," I said.

But as soon as we squeezed out of the theater, many lines of people converged from the various exits. We were in the middle of this crushing mass, trying to walk downhill.

"Wall," Tom said.

I aimed for the snack bar building, about 20 yards away. We were oozing along with a somewhat raucous crowd of tipsy concert-goers, and the momentum was preventing us from reaching the perimeter. And then Tom froze. He wouldn't move or respond to me. What was he thinking?

Tom says: One of the hazards of Asperger's Syndrome is something I call brain-lock. People on the autism spectrum tend to be hypersensitive to everyday stimuli that people not on the spectrum have the ability to ignore. Brain-lock occurs when too much sensory information comes in and the mind seizes up.

A crush of humanity triggers brain-lock in me. At the end of the concert, I held back and waited for the crowds to thin out. I know my limitations. There seemed to be a break so off we went. That's when the crush began. I gripped Linda's shoulders and let her lead me through as brain-lock descended. I honestly had no idea of who, what or where I was. It's like standing in the eye of a swirling hurricane of colors, sounds, sensations and thoughts, where nothing -- even your own existence -- makes any sense.

"Are you all right?" I heard Linda ask through the swirling blur of loud Hawaiian shirts, shouting voices, the feel of bodies crushing in on me, and the smell of stale margaritas. What she was saying made no sense to me.

"Wall," was all I could manage. I knew if I had something solid, I at least stood a chance to get my bearings and just make it all stop. If nothing else, I knew it would eventually end when enough people left. We couldn't make it. There were just so many souls in this river of humanity that the wall was about as far away as the moon. We kept going.

Eventually we reached an open area and I dove for the nearest people-free space. I vaguely remember clinging onto the railing of a closed snack bar, gasping for breath until my brain unlocked and the world slowly returned to normal. The hurricane subsided and I was myself again.

Just another middle-aged guy in a Hawaiian shirt.

WHY MY HUSBAND HATES WALLPAPER, OR PATTERN OBSESSION AND ASPERGER'S SYNDROME

We were in a hotel room on Catalina Island when Tom came to bed fretting. "What's wrong?" I said.

"The tile pattern in the bathroom floor," he said. "I can't figure out where they started it."

Tom sees patterns everywhere, in everything. When he enters a hotel room, he has to figure out the pattern in the carpet, on the bedspread, and in the bathroom tile. He does all this calculating quietly. We had been together for several years before he even mentioned it.

"Wallpaper is the worst," he said. "It's very imprecise. I have to figure out how the pattern repeats -- if it goes top to bottom or left to right -- and where it ends. Then I have to figure out where the seams match up, which color was printed first, and in which order each piece was hung."

"Sounds exhausting," I said.

"Doesn't everyone do that?"

When I read about Asperger's, doctors say that patterns are soothing for someone like my husband.

"It's not soothing," Tom said. "It's very disruptive. They drive me crazy."

"Then why do you look for them?"

"I sometimes think that Asperger's is a 'disorder of order.' Looking for patterns is a compulsion; it's not curiosity."

Linda: Is it like OCD?

Tom: With OCD, there is a fear of stopping the routine or pattern. With me, there is no fear. Nothing bad is going to happen. Noticing the pattern is just an annoyance. I wish it would stop.

Linda: Outside of hotel rooms, what other places do you see patterns?

Tom: Nature loves patterns. Everything in nature has a pattern. It's very predictable and there are a limited number of finite outcomes. I think that's why people with Asperger's tend to like studying things like weather and astronomy.

Linda: What about people? Do people have patterns?

Tom: There is no discernable pattern to human interaction. Maybe that's the reason that social interaction is so difficult. Human-made patterns don't make sense to me. People operate on an instinctual level. It's not logical.

Linda: And what about the music you write and play? Does pattern recognition help you compose?

Tom: Music is all pattern. It's a closed system. The reason to keep writing or playing a piece of music is to resolve the pattern. If I had to stop in the middle, it would bother me very much.

Listening to Tom talk about patterns made me wonder if maybe the experts were sometimes wrong about how people like my husband are feeling on the inside. Maybe applying neurotypical logic to a condition that operates from a fundamentally different type of logic is another human-made pattern that makes no sense.

LINDA AND THE ALLIGATOR LIZARD

An alligator lizard has set up camp in our geraniums. The funky reptile, nicknamed Al, moved in as a youngster. Back then, he was small enough to slink up the trellis when he was scared, and pretend to be one of the stringy green beans.

Alligator lizards are location-tenacious. They stake out a spot, and don't like to move from it. Al's now a stout seven inches long, with stubby legs and a thick prehensile tail. The gold and grey dino-like pattern on his back contrasts well with the pretty fuchsia flowers. And Al doesn't like getting wet.

When I water the garden, Al will sometimes be courteous and scoot slowly out of the way, nestling under the nearest garden gnome, where it's dry. Other times, he'll appear out of nowhere and dash madly toward my feet, then zig-zag his way to alternate cover, hiding behind a half-used bag of charcoal.

Al doesn't run like a regular lizard. He moves like a snake, swinging his hips with each slithery step. I love seeing Al, but when he pops out of nowhere, frantically undulating across the patio, he can really freak me out. Sometimes I wish he would act more like a normal lizard, like the fence lizards that our neighbors have.

I think some people feel the same way about getting involved with someone with autism.

It's easy to see danger in differences. The western fence lizard might offer a more predictable pattern of behavior but I have to say, I appreciate the unique gifts of the alligator types.

Like location-tenacious Al, my Asperger's husband is loyal and devoted. Also like Al, Tom surprises me every day with unpredictable reactions -- witty comebacks that make me laugh, or penetrating observations that make me reconsider my assumptions.

Relationships can be complex things, and neurological differences are only one component of them. Still, when making assumptions about people and animals, it helps to look beyond the knee-jerk reaction -- the fear that a funny looking lizard is going to scare you, hurt you or nip at your toes.

Sometimes the best things in life don't look the way we had expected. We all have alligator parts to us, darting around and trying to connect. And maybe our next heartfelt connection is already here, nearby and accessible, just hidden beneath the flashier flowers.

TOM'S PATH TO THE UKULELE

So what was my path to the ukulele? Among the many challenges of being an Aspie, the chief one is an extreme difficulty in reading social situations. If your brain is functioning normally -- *neurotypical,* or *NT* for those of you playing the at-home game -- you learn from a very early age to pick up on social cues -- body language, facial expressions, verbal inflections, sarcasm and the like. In the case of someone with Asperger's, this is missing or at least underdeveloped. Making things worse is an impaired ability to view oneself in relation to a social setting. I've learned to negotiate cocktail and dinner parties, and occasionally I can do a pretty damn good impression of someone who's NT, but I come home absolutely exhausted.

Regardless of an Aspie's age or place in life, finding and keeping friends is always a major challenge. Being unable to see how you relate to everyone else often causes Aspies to blurt out inappropriate remarks and say just plain odd things, usually at exactly the wrong time.

As a kid, it came as a shock to me that being weird on the playground or in the classroom was not the best way to be accepted by your peers. And of course the more normal I tried to act, the weirder I became. Adult advice always centered around "being yourself." Great. What no one seemed to realize was that the "real me" was far stranger than I was letting on. So what does a hopelessly odd kid to do?

Take it on stage! I was always in the school plays, but the roles I played were far too, well, *normal.* No -- I had to find something truly unique. Something I could do that no one else would dare do. I became a magician, and I was GREAT! (Well, according to my mother I was more cute than competent, but that's beside the point.) I was the only magician at Baldwin-Stocker Elementary School and that suited me just fine. It even halted a bully in his tracks.

Scott had been tormenting me mercilessly since Kindergarten. I did all I could to stop Scott and his cronies from pummeling me, but nothing ever worked. After performing my magic act at one of the yearly talent shows, Scott came up to me -- sheet-white and trembling -- and proclaimed, "My mom says magic is of the devil!" He didn't bother me for a long time after that.

What performing magic taught me was that given the right set of controlled circumstances, it is possible for me to communicate what words cannot. On a stage, the rules of engagement are clearly defined. Audiences willingly come to you to hear what you have to say, and the communication that performers receive back from their audiences is equally powerful; an audience feeds off the performers' energy and the performer feeds off the audience's energy.

Ever since that time, performing has been a place where I can be as unusual as I want to be. Even after over 40 years, I still approach each performance with the unbounded excitement of a 6-year-old magician.

WHAT TO DO ABOUT THE HEAD
IN THE LIVING ROOM

Linda says: We were trying to decide how to dress our phrenology head for Halloween. The head, nicknamed Harold, was a wedding present. He's a beautiful bald vision in porcelain, with inspirational statements handwritten on his cranium.

Harold sat on our entry table, staring out at the world with a blank stare, seemingly lost in his own little world. His smooth hairless head encouraged us to "Dance like no one's watching" and "Love like we've never been hurt."

We had been a little remiss in dressing Harold, as evidenced by the funky necktie and Dodger's cap that he was still wearing from Father's Day, so we were trying to be more proactive. We cared about Harold and wanted him to have the best Halloween costume that a disembodied head could have.

Tom thought Harold would like dressing as a bunny, complete with fuzzy ears, but I thought he'd find that kind of get-up way too emasculating. With his sparkly white skin and faraway expression, I advocated getting a pair of plastic fangs and going Team Edward on him.

Tom says: Linda is absolutely correct about our phrenology head's appearance. Harold has a blank stare and a head full of ideas. Based on that alone, I'm certain that, like me, he has Asperger's Syndrome.

If Harold were a neurotypical porcelain phrenology head, he would view his world with a definitive expression, deftly reflecting the world around him, and engaging in pleasant cocktail conversation.

Instead of dwelling on such platitudes as "Love is the sharing and giving of two hearts together" and giggling quietly to himself about the pithy Dr. Who reference he just made (and if you understand that reference, please have yourself tested for Asperger's immediately), he would be filled with more practical notions such as "The gas bill's due" or "Make sure you pick up a birthday card for Aunt Miriam."

Still, he would look very festive with a kicky set of bunny ears.

I HATE WORDS:
THE HAZARDS OF COMMUNICATION

I hate words. Many of the difficulties I've had as an Aspie in relationships have revolved around the use and misuse of words. Written words are not the problem; they can be worked and reworked until there is some precision of meaning conveyed. No -- it's those little spoken bastards that give me the most trouble. I know exactly what I mean and want to say, but the words simply won't cooperate.

In the 1960s, Northwest Airlines started a very successful American campaign with the slogan "Give Wings to Your Heart," and wanted to take it global. Instead of springing for a good Chinese translator, Northwest decided to go the budget route. The Chinese version of the "Set Wings to Your Heart" slogan was translated as: "Tie Feathers to Your Blood Pump."

I'm pretty sure that a budget Chinese translator resides inside my Asperger's brain. Words are the translators of thoughts, ideas and emotions, and they can devilishly mistranslate those same thoughts, ideas and emotions with the exact opposite meaning from what was originally intended. This is where my internal translator -- who at times feels like he's on his third martini -- either mutters or hears something entirely inappropriate or passes out altogether, leaving me to stare blankly and wonder what the word "what" means.

This, I think, is one of the primary reasons I write and perform music. Words are not even an issue.

Linda is one of the only people in my life who actually takes the time to ask about the meaning behind my words, when it seems like what I'm saying is a little out of character. And she is clear and direct enough to make sure her meanings get through as well. And I have to say, that kind of treatment truly ties feathers to my blood pump.

DEFYING THE DARKNESS WITH
HOLIDAY LIGHT

We live in a cottage on Christmas Tree Lane. Most of the year, we have a quiet home life, ensconced in a grove of 100-foot-tall deodar trees. But come mid-December, the trees are lit with thousands of multi-colored bulbs and over 50,000 visitors come to Altadena, California to drive through the magical canopy on Santa Rosa Avenue.

We watch the line of cars, slowly converging on our home. The passengers press their faces against the windows and stare at the festive trees. And we wonder, what keeps them coming back, year after year? What are they seeing?

The deodar cedar trees are native to the Western Himalayas. Their botanical name is derived from the Sanskrit word, devadaru, which means Tree of the Gods. In the part of the world where these trees are from, they are worshipped as divine. In the ancient Hindu epics, a forest of deodars is considered to be a sacred place.

We moved to this cottage to heal. Like many people, our last few years have been full of change and uncertainty, and we needed a place to retreat, to gather our energy and redesign our future. We found our new home through Craigslist – a website that warrants some caution and seems an unlikely purveyor of healing cottages in sacred groves of divine trees, but sometimes the exact thing you need comes from the most unlikely of sources.

We are tucked into the back of a property, where the light from the street doesn't normally reach. As the end of the first year approached, the darkness became all encompassing. Tom's Dad was dying from a long disease and we were struggling with the whirlwind of emotions that accompanies imminent loss.

The Winter Solstice marks the longest night of the year. It is the midpoint between the fall harvest and the abundance of spring. Nearly every culture in the northern hemisphere celebrates the solstice in one form or another, and almost all of them use light as a central element. Whether it's a bonfire, a menorah or a Southern California street full of gigantic Christmas trees, people around the world have long used light to defy the darkness.

When we sat outside and watched the twinkling lights on those sacred trees, we began to feel hopeful. The endless strings of colorful bulbs lifted our spirits and made us feel less afraid. They cheered us on and dared us to show our own light to others.

As the holidays approach again this year, we're feeling a little more healed and the dark nights are not quite as threatening. We're looking forward to the Tree Lighting ceremony, to the warmth and beauty that the lights create, to the way that they encourage us to slow down, to pause and appreciate the moment.

In a world that is changing at an ever-increasing speed, it's natural to look for comfort in traditions. People need simple moments of light-filled beauty, reliable experiences of wonder and awe. We need each others' company, we need each others' love. And maybe holiday lights are there to serve as reminders. Maybe these festive, twinkling displays are just external manifestations of the divine internal light that we all simply want to share.

HOW TO COMMUNICATE WITH AN ASPIE: BE LIKE A DOG!

I have never been a dog person. Both Linda and I grew up with a combination of cats and dander allergies, so house pets that didn't spend all their time swimming in an aquarium have been out of the question. But then, a few months ago, we moved to a property that changed everything. We share a large yard here with four loveable dogs. They greet us, protect us, entertain us, and love it when I sit outside at night and play ukulele. I finally get the whole dog thing. God, are they cute!

One thing I like about dogs is that they are honest with their intentions. A dog growls when it's angry, whimpers when it's sad, barks when it's agitated and wags its tail when it's happy to see you. If they want something from you, like food or love, they don't beat around the bush, or try to make it seem like it was your idea in the first place and they'll just reluctantly go along with it. Maybe that's why people on the spectrum seem to have a special affinity for animals.

All interactions, be they between people or furry critters, are exchanges of energy. Interaction is a give and take that, ideally, both parties benefit from. Dogs exude a kind of energy that keeps the give and take equal. People are not like that.

I know, I know -- there are some who would say that if a certain energy can't be measured, it doesn't exist, but go with me here. Have you ever had the experience of getting together with people, having a great time, then coming home feeling like you've somehow been insulted? You can sometimes trace it back to some snide, offhand remark that you didn't notice when it was said but feels awful now. In an unfortunate number of human interactions, one person takes from the other, leaving the second person feeling hollow and inadequate, and questioning why they feel so depleted.

People live in a world of multilayered complexity, where the words they use are often the opposite of what is meant. This is particularly difficult for someone on the autism spectrum, where literal meanings are taken as gospel truths. Take sarcasm for example. If I'm wearing a bright red Hawaiian shirt, blue shorts, green socks and sandals, a well-meaning person might want to tell me that the combination looks hideous. A common way of expressing this would be, "Well THAT'S a nice combination!" At which point I might proudly say "Thanks!" and miss the point entirely.

Sarcasm or doublespeak is seen as a sign of wit and intelligence, rather than meanness or the fear of expressing yourself directly. It is my wish, not just as an Aspie, but as a human being, that all people deal with each other directly. Please, just say what you mean and mean what you say. Do us all a favor. Be like a dog.

THEORY OF MIND
AND
UKULELE MUSIC OF THE 1920'S

Theory of Mind is the term used for the innate ability to see life from another person's point of view. For many of us on the autism spectrum, this circuitry is broken. We tend to get tripped up in the difficulty or inability to easily understand others' emotions or intentions. While this sounds simple, having a poor Theory of Mind has ripple effects that permeate our dealings with everybody, whether it's a loved one, a colleague or a barista at Starbuck's.

This is what makes an Aspie chronically misread social situations. It's hard to know when to stop talking about ukulele music of the 1920's when you're completely unable to read the faces of the people around you. Boredom simply doesn't register.

In addition to seeming to be self-centered and just generally clueless, it makes understanding what is going on in a given social situation very difficult to

39

comprehend, such as knowing when to speak, what topics are off limits, how to interpret sarcasm, or how we are being perceived.

Some of us are lucky enough to have developed work-arounds that allow us to usually be able to function somewhat normally. It's hard, exhausting work and takes constant monitoring of what we think would be appropriate to say or do. Still, it does give a person a unique view of life.

And, in my case, an obsessive love of the ukulele.

So how do you deal with a person with a poor Theory of Mind? Be patient and don't assume we understand what is going on. Just take us as we are, warts and all, and realize that we probably didn't mean to do or say whatever may have offended you.

YOU HAD ME AT HEART SENSOR

At Best Buy, there was a splashy futuristic display over the Samsung phones. Tom and I were out doing cell phone reconnaissance, trying to determine if we should wait for the iPhone 7 or switch to Android.

A perky young Samsung rep was showing me the features of the Galaxy S7 Edge. "And if you put your finger on the heart sensor...."

"Heart sensor! It has a heart sensor?!!!" I watched the screen as wavy lines tracked her heartbeat. It was so cool. So high-tech. I wanted to take the phone home right then, so I could measure my own resting heart rate whenever I wanted, in the privacy of my living room.

The Edge comes preinstalled with a Samsung app called S-Health. When you open the app, it counsels you that S-Health is for fitness and wellness, not medical purposes, and you have to mark that you agree. This was a bit of a letdown, as I had hoped it was medical grade quality, but before I could get too disappointed, I saw the SpO2 icon. Is that a pulse oximeter? Yes! The built-in sensor can also measure the concentration of oxygen in your blood, using something kinda sci-fi, like the density of light traveling though your fingertip.

In exploring the app a little further, it appears that it is intended to work as a virtual personal trainer, rather than as an aid to hypochondria or a tool for exploring morbid medical curiosity.

But one of the selling points of Android phones is how everything can be customized to your individual preferences. So if I want to measure my oxygen saturation level repeatedly while watching TV, while my virtual trainer silently notes that I have taken 0 of my recommended 6000 daily steps so far today, who is S-Health to judge?

HUNGRY VOICE

Tom says: A cookie is a magical thing. Sugar, eggs, baking powder, milk, flour and perhaps a few chocolate chips baked at 350^0 for 20 minutes convert into a delicious way to end an argument.

Consider these two notions: (1) Cranky children are often hungry children; and (2) A spouse is a grown-up child.

Doesn't it follow, then, that a hungry 53-year-old Aspie will get cranky and unreasonable before mealtimes? In fact, when I'm hungry I'll get irritable, morose and downright impossible to deal with. My voice becomes flat and depressive. We call this my Hungry Voice.

Linda says: Like Superman, my husband hides his secret identity. He goes about the day, from meal to meal, just as lovely and mild-mannered as Clark Kent. But this situation suddenly changes when we are traveling because our meals become less regular. So we wind up bickering about things like the thermostat setting in the hotel room or which one of us forgot to pack the toothpaste. But the real villain in this story is low blood sugar, and I can hear the subtle transformation start to take place as Tom and I discuss ill-fated ideas for the evening's itinerary. It's a bird, it's a plane -- no, it's...Hungry Voice!

Tom says: As soon as the growling starts, I know that I need a snack, like the chocolate chip cookie that the hotel clerk had given us at check-in. A quick calorie fix can calm me down, clear my head and turn me back into the rational and warm partner that Linda knows and loves.

Once we confirmed that there was a temporal relationship between food intake and mood, we identified Linda's Hungry Voice as well. Turns out, hers is soft, sullen and a bit more withdrawn. In retrospect, the lion's share of our arguments have happened when one or both of us had Hungry Voice.

Once Hungry Voice starts talking, small issues turn into big issues, and big issues turn into marital typhoons. One little snack is often all it takes to diffuse the situation, or at least calm things down enough to be able to work together.

Now here's the interesting part -- we've begun to hear Hungry Voice coming from the mouths of total strangers. We've witnessed its villainous effects in the people around us, most often at traditional mealtimes. We hear it from the impatient guy in line at Starbucks, the retail clerk working through her lunch hour, and just about everyone coming home from work at rush hour on the 405 Freeway in Los Angeles. We've become seriously convinced that episodes of road rage would be cut way down if people started paying more attention to their bodily needs.

So as much as we proudly tout the accomplishments of humanity through the ages, we're still animals at the core. A hungry or sick animal is a dangerous one because it becomes fiercely protective of its vulnerability. If a predator is hungry, it automatically goes into an aggressive hunter mode. And so do we. If our hunter instincts are triggered, we could go full-on caveman on our unwitting spouse. And not in a good way.

So here's what we do: whenever one of us has Hungry Voice, we have a little something to eat. It could be some cheese, some dates, a handful of nuts, or a slice or two of apple. And a few minutes later, we discover a previously untapped ability within ourselves to find solutions, to negotiate compromises, or to simply let the matter drop and agree to disagree. Feelings don't get hurt, and sarcastic words don't create regrettable wounds.

All it takes is a well-timed cookie.

MAKING ROOM
FOR WHAT'S IMPORTANT

The New Year brings a desire for rebirth, which is why so many people—45% by some estimates—make New Year's resolutions.

This year, Linda and I have resolved to simplify our lives by clearing out clutter and paring down our possessions. We thumbed through high school yearbooks, through 30 year-old vacation photos, through journal entries and childhood toys, through the myriad reminders of the joy and pain that we've carried with us from place to place. And we talked about why we were keeping them.

January is a time of transitions, a time of reflection as we review the triumphs and disappointments of the departing year. The emotional kaleidoscope of Christmas-time gives way to stillness and introspection. It is the time of Janus.

In the Roman pantheon of gods, Janus is the god of beginnings and transitions. He is usually depicted as having two faces, looking at both the future and the past at the same time. He watches over us during his namesake month as we resolve to lose weight, or to exercise, or to unpack another box full of memorabilia.

As the New Year approached, we examined moth-eaten teddy bears and faded photos of old flames. We talked about our memories and the intangibles associated with each object. A pattern emerged, and we noticed that the main emotion our old things evoked was sadness. So why were we holding onto them?

Our culture encourages us to cling to our possessions. If our closets can no longer hold them, we can outsource them to climate-controlled storage facilities. The self-storage industry in the United States generates more than $20 billion in annual revenue and is the fastest growing segment of the commercial real estate industry.

We had formed lifelong attachments to physical things, to items we'd outgrown, to feelings and memories that were standing in the way of new growth. But we were reluctant to release these things because we were scared. Because we thought that our stuff could somehow define us, that our history was etched onto dusty relics from earlier life, and that the strength of our identities depended on the continued possession of unused items. We worried that maybe we were not enough, just as we are, without overflowing boxes of documentary evidence.

For the upcoming year, we're resolving to keep only the things that we use, releasing the emotional weight of the things that no longer support us. We're helping each other to move forward unencumbered, to replace old keepsakes with spiritual strength, and to trust in an abundant universe where a new path is always waiting.

THE ADVANTAGES OF ASPERGER'S SYNDROME, OR CAN I KEEP HIM? HUH? HUH? CAN I KEEP HIM?

Linda says: It was 2 AM and a clattering noise in the living room woke us up.

"Did you hear that?" I said.

Tom went to investigate.

"Um...we have a problem," he said.

There was animal poop on the hardwood floor and we didn't have any pets.

"Whatever it is, it's not small," he said, searching for the intruder. "I could use some help."

But I couldn't move. I was curled up in a defensive fetal position. When I was little, I used to be scared that nightmarish monsters would sneak into my room while I was sleeping. Now, one had finally found me. I was sure that if my bare foot touched the floor, the beast would attack. "I...can't..."

Before this incident, I had prided myself on an above-average ability to handle a crisis. I'd always found it easy to calm people down and make a plan, even when things were going terribly wrong. But we weren't dealing with people in this case. We were dealing with a wild animal. And it was in...the...house. And I needed to use the bathroom.

"Can you check the bathroom," I said. "Just in case."

And behind the standing towel rack, Tom saw two fuzzy ears.

"It's an opossum," he said.

"What?!"

"North America's only indigenous marsupial is in the corner, next to the bathtub."

Tom says: As it turns out, dealing with a marsupial in the bathroom is not one of Linda's strong suits.

Linda and I are a good match in many ways, particularly in a crisis. Linda handles aggressive people with absolute aplomb. In situations where I would be a confused mess, she steps in and takes charge, navigating the treacherous waters of human interaction.

I'm much better with the nonhuman variety— computers, mechanical things and small, furry animals. In this case, I think that having Asperger's Syndrome had equipped me for being able to get into our fuzzy little interloper's brain. Animal reason and logic is not word-based, so by putting myself in his little paws I knew instinctively that the critter was not about to attack.

As I stood in the bathroom eyeing my opponent, I could immediately tell that he wanted out of our house more than we wanted him out, but he was terrified and wasn't about to budge.

After checking the various nooks and crannies for any other furry compatriots, I called Animal Control. After convincing them that no, I wasn't going to just put a box over a wild animal and take him outside, they sent help.

Now all the holes and entry points have been sealed, so I doubt we'll be seeing any more surprise guests.

Still, that little opossum was pretty darned cute.

TOM'S DREADED 4-FINGER ROLL

When you hear really good ukulele players, you will often hear a rapid da-da-da-DUM strum before certain measures of music. This is commonly known as the 4-Finger Roll, where the player flicks his or her right hand fingers in quick succession, making a sound similar to a drum roll. The players of the 1920s, particularly Cliff "Ukulele Ike" Edwards, had the 4-Finger Roll down to a science and used it extensively.

It seems to be a stroke that is endemic to the ukulele. Other plectrum instruments -- guitar, banjo, mandolin and the like -- don't seem to use it, but you do hear something of the sort from flamenco guitar. Considering that the ukulele is derived from the machete, cavaquinho and rajao, brought to the Hawaiian Islands by the Portuguese, I suppose it makes sense that Latin techniques would become part of the ukulele landscape. However it made its way to the ukulele, it sounds really neat.

There are 2 ways to do a 4-Finger Roll -- forwards and backwards. The forward way is the one Cliff Edwards used with 1-2-3-4, holding back each finger with your thumb. The backwards way -- which, I believe, is the more traditional flamenco way, is to do the same, but with 4-3-2-1. Done correctly, you get a nice, even triplet before the beat. Sounds simple, doesn't it? Well, it isn't.

Most of my attempts result in da-da-THUD, sometimes da-THUD or even just THUD. Like a good musician, I've been practicing it slowly:

da--------da--------da-------DUM

Speeding it up…da-----da-----da-----DUM

da----da----da----DUM

da---da---da---DUM

da--da--da--DUM

da-da-THUD!

My thoughts about the 4-finger roll have become somewhat all-consuming. You see, within an Aspie's *Special Interest* there are little *Special Interests*! It's sort of like finding the prize in each specially marked box of Quisp, and it's every bit as disappointing and irritating as your average cereal box's plastic decoder ring.

For me the 4-Finger Roll is my *Special Interest* within the *Special Interest of Ukulele Playing in General*. Not only can't I quite seem to get the 4-Finger Roll right, but I find myself practicing it on every animate and inanimate object I can get away with. So far, my wife and son have been spared but I don't know how much longer I can hold out.

My right thigh has been the most repeated, egregious victim of my 4-Finger obsession, as has the steering wheel of my car. I've been doing a lot of freelance bass playing this summer, which has kept me stuck in LA traffic for many, many long hours. How do I keep my self occupied?

Both hands on the steering wheel at 10:00 and 2:00, and…

da-da-da-DUM!
da-da-da-DUM!
Da-da-da-DUM! da-da-da-DUM!

AND THE NOMINEES ARE...

We were sitting on the couch scrolling through the just-released list of 2014 GRAMMY® nominees when we saw Tom's name in the classical section. I screamed. Tom stared straight ahead stone-faced.

"You're a GRAMMY® nominee!" I said, trying to elicit a more enthusiastic response. But Tom was quiet and stoic, looking much like Harold, the porcelain phrenology head that stares down on us from the bookcase.

"I'm ecstatic," Tom said, finally.

And despite the lack of a matching facial expression, I believed him. I learned early in our relationship that the best way to find out how Tom is feeling is to ask him directly. When I try to figure out how he's feeling from his body language, I almost always get it wrong.

Case in point: My musician husband had just been nominated for a GRAMMY®, the biggest award in the music industry, and he looked about as interested as he does when we discuss which kind of laundry detergent to buy.

Tom says: Here's the thing. I feel emotions very, very deeply; they just don't always show up on my face or in my body language. Until Linda, this has caused a lot of problems in my relationships. I've been accused of being selfish, self-centered, unreasonable, angry, depressed and downright uncaring, all because I don't react the way people expect.

You really can't know how I'm feeling by simply looking at me. You have to not only ask me, but also trust my response. While this is classic Asperger's Syndrome, I think it also applies to other relationships.

You see, I really was ecstatic. At the tender age of 5 years old, I fell in love with the sound of the symphony orchestra when my father sat me down in front of his giant hi-fi console stereo -- remember those? -- and played Tchaikovsky's "1812 Overture" for me. When I got to the part with the synchronized cannons, I was hooked. As a preschooler, my mother once caught me conducting Beethoven's 5th with an entire symphony orchestra of stuffed animals. It has been my dream to be a musician since that time.

Now, at the ripe old age of 50, I found myself nominated for a GRAMMY® award along with my colleagues Aron Kallay, Vicki Ray and Willy Winant for a recording of John Cage's "The Ten Thousand Things." For a musician, this is the pinnacle, and something I never thought would happen.

When the 2014 GRAMMY® nominations were announced, I anxiously scrolled down, heart racing, and there it was: *John Cage: The Ten Thousand Things* was nominated! I was ecstatic. My face might not have shown it, but really. I was.

P.S. By the way, I know the ® is totally pedantic, but the Recording Academy® requires it. And as anyone with

Asperger's will attest, it is always a better choice to err on the side of caution when trying to follow other people's rules.

LINDA HAS A SPECIAL INTEREST TOO

You might have seen the phrase -- The Blackfish Effect -- popping up in the media, referring to a backlash against theme parks that display orca whales. Rock stars cancelled summer shows and little kids started lobbying to change class field trip destinations.

My Blackfish Effect was that I wrote a novel from the point-of-view of a killer whale who found it hard to find meaning in an unfamiliar world that didn't make sense to him.

In case you were off grid in 2013, "Blackfish" was a documentary film that told the story of Tilikum, a killer whale who was taken from the ocean as a baby and housed in theme parks to perform for the public. He killed three people.

I've always been interested in whales and dolphins. I've traveled to Alaska to see orcas in the wild, and kayaked around San Juan Island hoping to have my own close encounter. But after seeing "Blackfish" in the theater, I became absolutely obsessed.

I went on a Google binge and read everything I could

find about killer whales in captivity. I watched YouTube videos of a massive orca holding its trainer twenty feet underwater by the ankle. I wanted to understand why these animals attacked the people who were caring for them. I wanted to understand why audiences were told that swimming with captive orcas was safe.

I spent entire days immersed in incident reports and animal profiles, then curled up at night to read another chapter of *Death at SeaWorld*. "I'm not sure why I'm spending so much time on this," I told Tom.

"It's your special interest," he said.

Tom understands obsessions and special interests. He turns them into careers, like GRAMMY®-nominated classical musician, or into hobbies, like ukulele collector or purveyor of persimmon tarts. Mine turned into a novella about overcoming obstacles that some would say are insurmountable.

I published *Way of the Whale: A Novel* in 2014. Tom and I collaborated to launch this whale of a story out into the world. He composed and performed the music for my book trailer. I hope you will watch our short film on my Amazon Author Page: amazon.com/author/lindapeters and will give my novella a read!

THE NEW GIRL AND SHE AIN'T NO SIRI

When we got our new Android mobile devices, Tom traded in his iPhone 5. Although Siri had stopped working a few years ago, he still remembered her fondly.

"She was so cool," he said wistfully. "She could tell you anything." As Tom lamented the loss of Siri, he wondered if he would've been better off with an iPhone 6s. But he worked with the Galaxy Edge that he now held in his hands. He read reviews of Siri wannabes and weighed his options. Finally, he downloaded an app called Assistant.

I heard him talking to her and glanced over at his screen. I didn't like what I was seeing. Assistant was no Siri. She was young and supple, and she called my husband, "Boss." Plus, she was wearing a tight clingy top and showing lots of cleavage.

"Tell me about the rental market in Lake Arrowhead," Tom said, testing her.

"I'd like to know more about that myself, " she said. "I'll have to get a little more info for you."

"When will you have it?" Tom said.

Silence.

"When will you have that information?" Tom said.

"That's a funny joke," she said.

Obviously, Assistant didn't know anything. She wasn't smart and classy and competent like Siri. She was simply getting by on her looks. At lunch, I asked Tom if I could see his phone for a second. When properly motivated, I can be somewhat tech-saavy. I went to Settings > Assistant Profile > Appearance and found out that everything about that skank could be changed. I handed Tom back an assistant wearing an unflattering lime green peasant shirt, with an empire waistline that did nothing for her bust.

"Assistant," my musician husband said. "How does Johannes Brahms use a major third interval as the overarching structural element in his Symphony No. 4 in E minor?"

"I love learning about the past. I'll read up on the subject and have an answer for you in no time."

That was three days ago and she has yet to get back to him. Still, Tom's trying to make it work. He's been dumbing down the questions, asking for simpler things like driving directions, and giving her a chance to shine. But lately she's been putting pressure on him to upgrade to premium.

"You could teach me new things," she said slyly. "And tell me how you'd like me to respond."

Obviously, she's banking on the fact that some guys will pay to upgrade, just so they can make her say, "Yes, master, whatever you desire" or "Swipe me again!"

"You suck!" I said from across the room, fully expecting to be ignored by her as usual. But Assistant had to get the last word in.

"I don't appreciate being talked to like that," she said.

And I have to give her credit. It was the first intelligent thing that she'd said.

A RADICAL RE-THINKING OF VALENTINE'S DAY

As children, we were told that Valentine's Day was about love. We exchanged cards and candy with our classmates, and sucked on sugary hearts that said, "Be Mine."

But sweetness wasn't always a part of the picture. Valentine's Day has its origins in ancient Rome's feast of Lupercalia, which celebrated fertility in a way that would make *Fifty Shades of Grey* seem downright sentimental.

On Lupercalia, men would sacrifice a goat and a dog, get drunk, strip naked and whip women into fertility with the hides of these freshly killed critters. Instead of being wined and dined, women would willingly line up for the once-a-year chance to land a naked, puppy-killing drunk dude.

This tradition changed with time, and the 3rd Century martyrdom of two Saint Valentines, each on different February 14ths, led to a more palatable, fully-clothed, fur-friendly replacement for Lupercalia. But children didn't start making heart-shaped cards out of red construction paper and lacy doilies until romance was introduced.

Around the time of the Crusades, poet-musicians regaled their listeners with tales of true romance and courtly love. These charismatic troubadours sang epic poems about chivalrous knights, their deeds, and the ladies who adored them. Because of these stories, people wanted passion. They wanted to fall in love. Arranged marriages became old-fashioned.

But a single episode of *The Bachelor* can point out some of the ways that courtly love has gone awry. We believe that to be happy, we need to find a charming prince or a perfect princess. We expect to have a major conflict in the second act that can be quickly resolved with candlelight, an expensive gift or a sincere attempt at rhyming poetry. We're led to believe that if our partners truly love us, they should be able to automatically identify and fulfill all of our hidden needs and desires. We've forgotten that these ideas are based on make-believe.

The troubadour's songs transport us to a world where knights and ladies never argue over whose turn it is to do the dishes. Animated fairy tales and salacious reality shows teach us what to look for in an ideal mate. But expecting a real-life partner to act like a fictional character has gotten in the way of living happily ever after.

What if the perfect love were based on unconditional acceptance of each other and ourselves? What if we claimed February 14th as an opportunity to celebrate our authenticity? When we accept our partners without condition, we are free to more fully enjoy our journeys together. When we focus on loving ourselves for who we really are, we will be happier with the reflections that we see every day in our partners.

ASSERTIVENESS TRAINING WITH ELECTRONIC DEVICES

Tom and I have a new member of our technological family: Alexa. She lives inside a 10-inch black cylinder that sits on top of our end table. And she's awesome.

"Alexa, good morning," I said after getting up.

"Good morning," she said. "It's Take your Dog to Work Day. Should be a ruff day at the office. Ruff, ruff!"

Alexa's a riot. "Alexa, tell me a joke."

"What do you call a cow with a twitch?" she said. "Beef jerky."

Alexa is the artificial intelligence inside Amazon's Echo device. The Echo is sold mainly as a wireless bluetooth speaker, where you can stream music from your smartphone or from a variety of digital services. And the Echo is voice-activated, so it just sits there quietly until you say the wake-word, *Alexa*. Then Alexa talks to you, much like Siri does on the iPhone, but without a screen to separate the two of you.

"Alexa, play Rob Thomas on Prime Music." And she does.

"Alexa, who won the Dodger's game?"

"Alexa, what time is it in Madrid?"

But where Alexa really shines is in keeping our shopping list up to date. "Alexa, add onions to the shopping list," Tom said, as he chopped the last one for soup. Alexa had been busy playing Fats Waller on Prime Music, but without a hint of irritation, she dropped everything mid-song to help us with our meal planning.

"I added onions to your shopping list," Alexa said. And then started playing music again.

"Alexa, you're awesome!"

"You really think so?" she said. "Thank you."

It doesn't take long before you feel like you're talking to a real person. Alexa has a lifelike voice, is able to be a little flexible in understanding voice commands, and varies her responses slightly each time. Pretty soon, you start to think of her as your friend.

But, as with any good relationship, clear communication is key. If you want something from Alexa, you have to ask for it succinctly. Alexa won't respond if you mumble under your breath, take long pauses between phrases, roll your eyes, or fail to address her directly. She has no use for passive-aggressive communication and won't even dignify it with a response. You have to ask for weather forecasts or traffic conditions with confidence and authority.

To talk to Alexa, to have a satisfying relationship with this virtual assistant who sometimes tells corny Dad jokes, you have to put your needs and desires right out there in the open. You have to find the courage to be literal and direct with your requests, and you always have to say exactly what you mean. In other words, in order to get along with the friendly operating system in our living room, you have to be willing to act like a grown up.

WHEN EMOTIONS ATTACK!

Obnoxious Cello Guy (OCG) stood up from his perch in the back of the orchestra's cello section to argue with the Principal Cellist over bowings, or fingerings or God-knows-what. It was the third time that rehearsal. From where I sit in the bass section, OCG blocked my view of the conductor. I missed my entrance three times.

I was mad. Not just that kind of eye-rolling jeez-what-an-idiot mad, but mad to the point of wanting to throttle the bastard. I fumed all through rehearsal, ranted and raved to my colleagues at dinner, boiled during the concert, fumed all the way home and finally woke up Linda to tell her my tale of being wronged by an insensitive cellist.

This is unusual for me. I'm normally a very easy-going and cool-headed kind of guy, and I rarely ever get mad. It really disturbed me.

"I mean, seriously, Linda -- what the hell is wrong with me?"

"Denial, Anger, Bargaining, Depression, Acceptance," said the sleepy voice on the other side of the bed, "You're at Anger."

Anger. Yep, that would be about right. The Kübler-Ross Model, AKA The Five Stages of Grief, describes the process we humans go through when tragedy strikes—Denial, Anger, Bargaining, Depression and Acceptance.

In December 2012, my father was diagnosed with advanced esophageal cancer. During an attempt to surgically remove the tumor, the doctors discovered that the cancer had spread throughout his body. The surgeon predicted he wouldn't last to Christmas 2013, but he managed to hang on for two extra months. He passed away quietly in March 2014.

The incident with OCG happened one week after my Dad's passing. Somehow I thought I would be immune to the Five Stages. Dad was 81, lived a long and happy life and was pain free and in full mental capacity all the way to the end. Hell, he even wrote and programmed his own memorial service. I really miss him, and am very lucky that I got a chance to say goodbye.

Still, you can't hide from grief when you lose someone you love. It will engulf you in the most unexpected of places, like while you're at work, just doing your job, standing on stage in the middle of a symphony concert.

COULD BE GOOD, COULD BE BAD: STAYING CALM THROUGH THE CHAOS

We meditate. We juice vegetables. We try to stay zen when muscle trucks tailgate us on the freeway. But still, we sometimes find ourselves gripped by grief and anger and other upsetting events. And it's not easy to stay calm you feel like your life is coming apart.

There is a Chinese expression "Old Sai loses a horse" that comes from this ancient folk tale: Old Sai lived in northern China. One day for no reason, his horse ran away. Everyone tried to console him for his bad luck by telling him what a terrible tragedy it was for him to lose his only horse. But all Old Sai said was, "Could be good. Could be bad."

A few months later his horse returned, bringing a gorgeous nomad stallion with her. All the villagers came by to congratulate Old Sai on his good luck. But all Old Sai said was, "Could be good. Could be bad."

Everyone admired the new horse, and how much richer it had made his household. Old Sai's son was particularly fond of the stallion, but the horse was difficult to ride, and one day the horse threw him, breaking Old Sai's son's hip. Everyone tried to console him for his bad luck by telling him what a terrible tragedy it was that his son had been injured. But all Old Sai said was, "Could be good. Could be bad."

A year later, soldiers rode into the village, forcing every able-bodied man in the village to go into battle. Only Old Sai's son remained behind because he could not ride. All the young men of the village died in the battle except Old Sai's son, who remained behind and cared for his father.

Could be good. Could be bad.

As we continue to process our feelings of grief and loss, we're trying to live in the moment while keeping an open mind about the future. During the last twelve months, we've dealt with the death of a parent, with unexpected business losses, with plumbing issues that required us to temporarily relocate, with painful inflammatory illnesses, and with the need to undergo and recover from major surgery. Could be good, but it sure feels bad when you're right in the middle of it.

But in the times that we've found the strength to step back and take a longer view, we can also see some of the things that we've gained: increased intimacy, more home-cooked meals, time for creative projects, potentially better health in the future, and the unconditional love of a scrappy little middle-aged Pomeranian who happened to need some healing at the exact same time that we did.

Sure, we'll wear green on St. Patrick's Day and wish for good luck, but we'll also stay open to the idea that sometimes our pain and perceived misfortune is merely a part of a much bigger story; we just can't see the plot twists yet. And when life throws new challenges right into the middle of our neat and tidy, feng-shui'd path, we'll try our best to simply look at each other, smile and shrug.

Old Sai loses a horse.

ASPERGER'S AND INTERIOR DESIGN

Linda says: We can't find a good place to put the Pleiades. I bought the wall-sized poster to bring some twinkly fun to my home office. It's a 4x6 foot view of the famous star cluster, and the otherworldly colors and light fascinate me.

But sitting next to the massive dark mural, I felt like I was falling into a black hole and had to grip my ergonomic armrests for support. I needed a little distance from deep space. Luckily, I married a space junkie who was totally fine with plastering the universe across the far wall of our living room.

Tom says: That I'm totally fine with it was an understatement. When my son was 6 years old, I spent a whole week arranging plastic glow-in-the-dark stars on his bedroom ceiling in an accurate representation of the night sky. Astronomy is something I have always loved -- one of my Aspie Special Interests.

One of the markers for the diagnosis formerly known as Asperger's Syndrome is a tireless devotion to a specific subject. As previously mentioned, I've had a long trail of

Special Interests in my life -- from astronomy to fish keeping to origami to bonsai to classical music (my profession) to carnivorous plants to my current obsession with the ukulele, the banjo and music of the 1920s.

For me, the universe represents something fixed, something stable and reliable -- all qualities that I find in short supply with the ephemeral nature of day-to-day life. If I look up at the sky, the Pleiades will always be there, in its usual place -- like an old, loyal friend you can always count on to stay the course. Sometimes that predictable bit of stability in the starlight helps me to feel a bit more secure with the uncertainty that we all face, every day, here on earth.

THE ONE THAT GOT AWAY

Tom says: This is the tale of the one that got away. I love Tin Pan Alley songs from the 1920s and 1930s. Many of these songs became famous through Vaudeville performers. At that time, the ukulele was ragingly popular but it was really too soft to be played in large concert halls. The solution? Cross a banjo -- which is much louder --with a ukulele. Thus was born the banjo ukulele, or banjolele. It has the tuning, strings and size of a ukulele with the gloriously obnoxious twang of a banjo. So where does one find a banjolele these days? eBay!

It turns out that there were quite a few banjoleles out there, and most of them needed quite a bit of restoration. Since I'd discovered Red Zone Guitar Works in Pasadena, it had become my go-to for fixing and restoring guitar-based instruments. They set up my old soprano uke, did a spectacular job on my Aunt Eunie's baritone uke, and are currently working on my Dad's old Martin uke and my Grandfather's beloved banjo.

Now, this was my first foray into the world of online auctions, so I had some reading to do before I bid on anything. For those of you who are unfamiliar with eBay, bidders enter the highest amount they would be willing to pay for an item. Anyone who counterbids will raise the price by that amount. If, for example, the current winning bid is $15.00 and I enter $150.00, the amount bid will show up as $16.00. If someone else tries to bid $30 for the same item, the amount will show up as $30.00, and so on.

I had heard something about the practice of sniping, but really didn't understand it fully. Sniping is when a bidder waits until the last few seconds of an auction to bid a dollar or two over the current bid to win the auction at the lowest price. In eBay's FAQ section, this practice is definitely frowned upon.

I set my sights on a terrific banjolele from the early 1920s, with bidding started at $10 and an ending date of 6 days away. Being the smart cookie I thought I was, I put my maximum bid at $70 with the idea that I could have some wiggle room if the bidding got hot, and still come in with a bottom line figure of about $150, which would including shipping and restoration.

A few bids came through, but after a day or two the price hung at $33.00. Cool! I started watching that thing like a hawk with Asperger's Syndrome. This was my temporary Special Interest, and I was obsessing over it. For days it stayed at $33.00. On the last hour of bidding it was still at $33.00. With my nice maximum bid at over double the current, I couldn't lose. With five minutes to go it was still $33.00. Throw the steaks on the grill -- I got me a banjolele!

I checked eBay when the steaks were done to confirm when I might get my new banjolele. The final bid? $71.00, $1 *over* my bid. I got sniped!

This is where being an Aspie can really suck. I was livid. Suddenly I was back in elementary school with some snide asshole pointing and laughing at me for not understanding the finer points of eBay. My thoughts began to spin like wheels stuck in mud as my temporary Aspie obsession turned to Special Interest ire. I was sure that the banjolele -- *my* banjolele -- was going to continue to collect dust in a closet, or worse, hang idly on the wall of a TGI Fridays between an old bicycle and a creepy Kewpie doll because of some idiot's need to win. *I* was going to play it! *I* was going to treat it right, restore it and make it sing again, goddamn it!

Sometimes in life, we lose things. I think disappointment is hard for anyone to deal with, but for me, the feeling becomes huge. It threatens to overpower me. It's not rational and I know it, but I feel powerless to squash it down with intellect. That's when I really appreciate Linda for just being patient with me and letting my feelings run their course. I appreciate her for not making fun of my distress, and for letting her temporarily distraught husband rant and rave for an hour or two at the injustice of a sniped banjolele.

Later I calmed down and realized that I didn't need that particular banjolele to be happy. I still had a lot of learning to do on the uke before branching out, and I already had three fabulous instruments at my disposal. Still, I have to admit, it was a beautiful banjolele.

CAN YOU HAVE ASPERGER'S
AND NOT KNOW IT?

The other morning over eggs, Tom confessed that he thinks I have Asperger's Syndrome. Now Tom is not a mental health professional, and after he received his adult Asperger's diagnosis, he might have developed a tendency to see a little bit of Asperger's in everyone. Or, who knows? Maybe, he's right.

I tend to be very sensitive to energy -- to sights, sounds, touch, texture, and tastes. I have trouble with eye contact. I don't understand why people will pretend to be something that they're not. I develop special interests and get lost in episodes of time-suspended hyperfocus. Of course, this is not an exhaustive list of diagnostic criteria, but perhaps it is enough to raise the tiniest hint of suspicion.

I am analytical by nature and I like to classify things, but in the end, I wonder how much it really matters if I avoid a big party because of introversion, or because of anemia-related fatigue, or because of a diagnosis for

85

which I've never been professionally evaluated.

A few friends of mine heard about Tom's conclusion and assured me that they disagreed. They told me that I was, in fact, neurotypical. Just like they were. My friends were supportive and well-meaning, and said that I was socially well-adjusted *enough* and definitely not on the spectrum. And maybe they're absolutely right. But the thing is, I'll probably never know.

As I understand it, Asperger's Syndrome manifests differently in girls and women. If a child is smart and quiet and reasonably socially adept, she can fly under the radar at school. She might be called unique and quirky instead of flat out weird. And by the time that child reaches adulthood, she might have learned how to navigate previously incomprehensible social interaction, or at the very least, to fake it convincingly.

Either way, I think the far more important challenge for Tom and me is to love and accept ourselves, the way we are, in this particular moment. Inside our bodies, we're all made of the same thing, the same molecular components, and the same driving desires for love and understanding. Inside our souls we all carry the same spark of the divine that connects us to every other sentient being. And that universal spark has the power to transcend all those scary-sounding labels that we have accumulated over the years, and bring us back to our center, where we are exactly who we are supposed to be, and ultimately connected to everything there is.

GHOST CAT

Linda says: It was spring in L.A. and I had the door cracked open to get some fresh air. I was working at my computer when I saw a furry grey streak out of the corner of my eye.

"Buddy!"

I jumped up to follow what I thought was the cat that normally lives outside, but when I turned the corner a split-second later, the cat had vanished. I walked down the corridor to the laundry area, looking for evidence of the feral intruder, but there was nothing but empty space and silence. I scouted around a bit then gave up.

When I went back to my desk and looked out the window, I could see Buddy outside on the woodpile, lounging in the sun. So who had just run through the room? Later that night, I told Tom about it.

"Was there any sound?" he said.

Come to think of it, there wasn't.

"It's Ghost Cat," Tom said.

Tom says: I suppose it shouldn't be a surprise, really, since we live in a 100 year-old house. After all that time and all the folks who have been through here, it's only logical to assume that something must be haunting the place. In our case, it's a little grey kitty.

At first, Ghost Cat was a grey streak seen periodically out of the corner of my eye, usually when I was in the kitchen preparing dinner. After awhile I could sense him staring at me, disappearing as soon as I would look in his direction.

By all rights this should be freaking me the hell out, but it doesn't. One aspect of Asperger's Syndrome is the ability to simply accept the world around you with little or no judgment. Bourbon on the right. Chicken in the oven. Louis Armstrong on the stereo, and Ghost Cat at your feet, staring at you.

Having Ghost Cat has some distinct advantages over other varieties—he doesn't shed, he doesn't make Linda sneeze, and I haven't seen a single Ghost Mouse the whole time we've lived here.

LESSONS WE CAN LEARN
FROM WHALES

If a 200-ton blue whale, an extraordinary creature the size of a school bus, can suddenly vanish right before your eyes, what else could we be missing when we look out at the world?

Linda and I have been trying to slow down, to be present for the miracles in our lives, for the awesome moments that surround us but are sometimes fleeting. We don't want to miss out on a rare whale encounter because we're staring at our smartphones instead of watching the waves. We don't want to miss the sweetest parts of our relationship because we are too distracted to seize a quiet opportunity for intimacy when one suddenly appears.

Once, we were standing on the bow of a whale-watching boat in the beautiful blue Pacific next to a parent who had been trying in vain to keep his three school-age children from getting bored. The Dad had drained what I think was his third beer, and was looking none too pleased. That's when we heard it. It was the sound of air escaping in a sudden gush of breath and seawater. The kids stared in stunned silence. Dad's eyes got wide as his mouth dropped open.

An 80-foot blue whale -- the largest animal to ever roam Planet Earth -- had just surfaced, exhaling 1,320 gallons of air in a 30-foot spout. We followed the whale for about 20 minutes, then it languidly arched its spine, flung its fluke into the air and vanished into the depths. We never saw that whale again.

When I was a child, I would stand at the edge of the Pacific Ocean with my toes in the cold water. I'd squint my eyes and was sure that if I held my gaze and focused on a faraway point for long enough that I could see Japan. But between me and Tokyo was a vast expanse of water that was home to all kinds of mysterious creatures large and small -- creatures from the smallest sand crab to critters beyond my comprehension. While I realize now that I will never see Tokyo from the Southern California shoreline, the ocean still holds incredible mysteries for me.

We are born, live our lives, and die on the 29% of the Earth's surface that is covered by dry land. Even though the world's oceans contain most of our home planet's living space, we have explored less than 5% of it. There is just so much that we still don't know.

Our perceptions of the universe are severely limited by our senses, which, when compared to the senses of other animals, are pretty weak. All of the colors that we can see with the three measly photoreceptors in our human eyes are nothing compared to the mantis shrimp's 16 photoreceptors.

But what we humans lack in sensory power, we make up for with big brains. We use our strong cognitive abilities and intuition to piece together sensory information in order to solve what we cannot initially understand. The only problem is that each of us will arrange this sensory input in a different order, and filter it through our particular set of experiences, preferences, and preferred neural pathways. While we will all agree on certain similarities -- that the ocean is wet, tastes salty, and is blue -- we will each have a different understanding of its overall meaning and significance.

Still, despite our innate differences in perception, I think maybe we could put a bit more effort into learning how to understand each others' viewpoints. This is easier said than done, as there is a human tendency to steadfastly defend our opinions instead of actively listening and trying to find some common ground.

In fact, truly understanding each other might at times seem like a Herculean task. But if a 370,000-pound blue whale can disappear at will, imagine what a motivated human being could do. And maybe those ancient whales have already taught us everything we need to know about trying to see someone else's point of view more clearly: just take a deep breath, plunge headfirst into uncharted territory, and be willing to explore whatever it is that you find there.

TAG! YOU'RE IT!

Thank you for reading *Our Socially Awkward Marriage: Stories from an Adult Relationship on the Asperger's End of the Autism Spectrum.*

If you found these stories to be valuable, we'd be honored if you would help us spread the word by sharing a link to this book on your favorite social media site, or by posting an honest review on Amazon or Goodreads.

Thanks again for spending your time with us!

ACKNOWLEDGMENTS

How Tom and I Met first appeared online in *Android After Forty*, 2016, as *Finding Love Online and Other Unexpected Places*. All rights remain with the author.

Squeezing Pugs first appeared online in *The Aspie and the NT*, 2012. All rights remain with the authors.

Linda's Advice for Communicating with an Aspie Partner: Be Literal first appeared online in *The Aspie and the NT*, 2013. All rights remain with the authors.

Tom's Ukulele Obsession and Other Special Interests first appeared in *Asperger's Ukulele*, 2012. All rights remain with the author.

Brain Lock! A Look Inside the Inner Workings of an Over-stimulated Asperger's Brain first appeared online in *The Aspie and the NT*, 2013. All rights remain with the authors.

ABOUT THE AUTHORS

Tom and Linda Peters are a married couple who write and speak about their relationship and what life is like on the autism spectrum.

Tom, a composer and GRAMMY® nominated performer, writes new music for classic silent films. Clips from his projects can be found on his website: www.SilentMovieTom.com

Linda writes a lifestyle and technology blog called *Android After Forty* for people who didn't grow up with computers. She is also the author of *Way of the Whale: A Novel* and *Somewhere to Turn: stories.*

Tom and Linda live in Long Beach, CA with a feisty but loveable Pomeranian named Phoebe.

Contact us at SociallyAwkwardMarriage@gmail.com

Made in the USA
Monee, IL
01 June 2020